Create the Life You Want

How to Attract Health, Wealth,
Happiness and Peace of Mind
Using the Religious Science
of Raymond Charles Barker

Create the Life You Want

How to Attract Health, Wealth,
Happiness and Peace of Mind
Using the Religious Science
of Raymond Charles Barker

by

Raymond Charles Barker

*Compiled and Edited and Updated
for the 21st century
by
William F. Shannon*

Hudson Mohawk Press
Latham, NY

Hudson Mohawk Press LLC
595 New Loudon Road #138
Latham, New York 12110

www.hudsonmohawkpress.com
www.facebook.com/hudsonmohawkpress

Compilation, introduction, editing, and updating
copyright © 2013 by Hudson Mohawk Press LLC

All rights reserved.

This edited and updated compilation first published in the United States in 2013 by Hudson Mohawk Press LLC. Portions previously appeared in different form in *Miscellaneous Writings of Raymond Charles Barker* (1958) and *Money Is God in Action,* published by First Church of Religious Science, New York. "Life as a Creative Experiment" and "The Necessity of Creative Ideas" previously appeared in different form in *The Science of Successful Living* (1957), published by Dodd, Mead, New York. This work is not published by the original publishers of *Miscellaneous Writings of Raymond Charles Barker*, *Money Is God in Action*, or *The Science of Successful Living* or by their successors.

The text of this updated edition has been edited into gender neutral language, except when to do so would render the text awkward for the reader.

ISBN 978-0-9843040-9-7 (paperback)
eISBN 978-1-940124-00-1

Library of Congress Control Number: 2013941598

Book design by William F. Shannon

CONTENTS

Introduction	i
Each Person Is a Spiritual Potential	1
A Higher Mountain	3
The World Needs You	5
Your Great Opportunity	7
The Faith That Demonstrates	9
The Necessity of Courage	11
The Vitality of Creative Thought	13
Mind Is Your Security	15
Mental Efficiency	17
A Modern Definition of God	19
The Finger of God	21
The Immediacy of God	23
Where Are You Going?	25
The Divine Economy	27
The Availability of Wisdom	29
Each Person Is God's Representative	31
I Live With Expectancy	33
The Infinite Thinker	35
There Is a Goodness	37
Watch Your Mind	39
The Directed Mind	41
Mind Inspires Each of Us	43
You Are a Free Agent	45
The Supreme Statement of Life	47
The New Is Appearing	49
The Power to Accomplish	51
You Need a Spiritual Basis	53
The Attitude Which Prospers	55
The Right-Minded Prosper	57
The Determining Factor of Thought	59
A Year of Greatness	61
The Victory of Easter	63

Be Thankful	65
The Real Meaning of Christmas	67
Life as a Creative Experiment	69
The Necessity of Creative Ideas	71
Money Is God in Action	83
A Spiritual Mind Treatment for Money	93
A Spiritual Mind Treatment for Prosperity	95

INTRODUCTION

by
William F. Shannon

This book is a collection of writings by Raymond Charles Barker, one of the most popular exponents of New Thought in the mid-20th century. Many of the essays included here have been out of print and unavailable for many years. Other material is available here for the first time edited into gender neutral language for the 21st century, making Barker's ideas freshly accessible to a new audience.

Barker had a unique ability to explain in a clear and simple way metaphysical ideas like the law of attraction, affirmations, meditation, mental healing of the body, and what he termed "spiritual mind treatment". He inspired many people to take charge of their lives and change in positive ways. He spoke not only in the United States but also around the world, emphasizing over and over how the power of thought can be used to heal the body, mind and spirit, and thus eliminate fear, anxiety, worry, nervousness, pessimism and unbelief. Barker was adamant that everyone could benefit from putting these principles into practice in their lives. He touched the lives of thousands through his lectures and writings.

By following Barker's advice, we can treat the subconscious blocks that prevent us from attaining our goals. We can create new ideas, eliminate problems, create happiness for ourselves and others, remove the belief of lack and limitation, and learn how to decongest our consciousness and create a fresh mind.

* * * * *

For those who are not familiar with the "Religious Science" to which Barker refers throughout this book, perhaps a brief discussion is in order. Religious Science has nothing to do with the controversial Church of Scientology or the very unique Christian Science Church founded by Mary Baker Eddy (although Mary Baker Eddy got many of her ideas from early New Thought practitioners). Rather, Religious Science is a branch of the New Thought movement founded in 1927 by Ernest Holmes (1887-1960). Religious Science is now more commonly referred to as Science of Mind, operating under the umbrella organization Centers for Spiritual Living.

In founding Religious Science, Ernest Holmes was influenced by earlier New Thought writers and practitioners, including Emma Curtis Hopkins (with whom he studied), Phineas Parkhurst Quimby, Thomas Troward and the transcendentalist Ralph Waldo Emerson. Before going out on his own Holmes was ordained a minister in Divine Science, another branch of the New Thought movement. Publication in 1926 of his classic book, The Science of Mind, served as a catalyst for organizing this new branch of the movement. In The Science of Mind, Holmes developed

Introduction

his own particular synthesis of New Thought ideas, culminating in the establishment of the Church of Religious Science, which would become Centers for Spiritual Living.

Religious Science's version of affirmative prayer is known as spiritual mind treatment. Barker discusses spiritual mind treatment throughout this book, and two useful spiritual mind treatments are provided after the section entitled "Money Is God in Action."

Religious Science has many ideas and concepts in common with the other branches of the New Thought movement. Here is a summary of the core concepts of Religious Science/Science of Mind:

(1) There is one indestructible, absolute, self-existent Cause that manifests Itself through all creation -- commonly called God.

(2) We are all individualizations of the One Spirit, of this One Cause.

(3) Law is continuously set in motion by our thoughts, which in turn find their source in God.

(4) All conceivable Good is eternally available to us, ready to flow into our experience. The flow of Good is activated and/or increased by our belief, faith, and acceptance. The expression of this essential belief, faith, and acceptance is prayer, or spiritual mind treatment.

(5) This is a Universe of Wholeness, Allness, and Oneness. Nothing operates in isolation.

(6) This is a Universe of infinite spiritual, mental and physical abundance, which can never be depleted. There is always more than enough.

(7) For everything visible, there is an invisible counterpart. Everything in nature tends to equalize itself, to keep its balance true.

(8) The Universe exists in the Eternal Now, each moment complete and perfect within itself. In this Universal Harmony, justice without judgment is always automatic, an infallible Universal Principle. There can be no place for Divine anger, unforgiveness, or punishment.

(9) God knows only Life, its eternal continuity, evolution, and expansion. Thus, the individual soul is eternal, immortal and continuous, forever expanding.

(10) The Christ is a principle, a Universal Presence, not a person. It is the Universal Image of God present in all creation and in all people, and is always available to assist in our positive personal evolution, and the positive evolution of society.

* * * * *

Raymond Charles Barker (1911-1988) studied at the Unity School of Christianity in Lee's Summit, Missouri and was ordained a Unity minister in 1940. After serving as minister at the Unity Center in Rochester, New York, he became affiliated with the Religious Science movement. At the request of Ernest Holmes, Barker opened the First Church of Religious Science in New York City in 1946. He was President of the International New Thought Alliance from 1943 to 1946, and was President of Religious Science International from 1954 to 1957 and 1959 to 1962. (Religious Science International became the organization that merged with a sister organization in 2011 to form Centers for Spiritual Living, more commonly known as Science of Mind.) Barker's deep involvement in both Unity and Science of Mind gave him a unique perspective on the New Thought movement and allowed him to synthesize ideas from

Introduction

different streams into his own particular blend. His students included Louise Hay and Stuart Grayson.

* * * * *

WILLIAM F. SHANNON is the Publisher and Editor of Hudson Mohawk Press. He holds a Master of Arts in Integrated Studies/Cultural Studies from Athabasca University in Canada.

EACH PERSON IS A SPIRITUAL POTENTIAL

The last one hundred years[*] have brought forth a new concept of the person. Religious Science has played an important role in this revelation. It has steadfastly proclaimed that each person is a spiritual potential whose full nature warrants our exploitation. Psychology explores the negatives of the human mind. Religious Science explores the spiritual resources of the individual, yet, it uses psychological techniques to do this.

Each person is a powerhouse of mental dynamite. Our use of mind determines our experience. Viewing our mind merely as a human we behold problems, world conditions and limitations. From the spiritual side of things, we see what we can be, even if we haven't yet become it. God never limits us. We have accepted our own limitations by knowing more facts about more things. But, we now discover that more facts about more things do not produce a better person or a better world. They only produce more comfort.

The new person as studied by Religious Science is a growing spiritual experiment. And, this experimentation is one of mind action. Facts are ideas completed. Each person is cause and by our causation we determine the facts which will take place. Our motives determine our desires. Our desires stimulate our emotions. Our emotions give rise to the direction of

---

[*] *Editor's Note*: Barker is writing in the mid 1950s.

1

our thinking. Our thinking causes the Law of Mind, the subconscious, to produce form.

This entire process is a spiritual one, because God is all in all. We believe this and we prove this. The traditional thinkers neither know it, nor can they receive the benefits from knowing it. So, they struggle to achieve, while we rest in a Law that does the work for us. The new Person knowing themselves as God in action works effortlessly in bringing to pass the desires of their heart.

Our technique is simple. We affirm our thinking process to be divine. We know that what we think and feel causes a subconscious Law to act and bring forth a result. Religious Science is a light unto the world. It reveals what each person can be. It does not emphasize our errors. It keeps its sights on the God-person and teaches us to grow into our true stature.

A HIGHER MOUNTAIN

Mind moves each person forward. Spirit impels us to greatness. Law brings to pass our decisions. This is Religious Science. But, Religious Science can be demonstrated only by people who know who they are and where they are going. It is not a philosophy; it is a science. It is not a theology; it is a practice. The brave accept its challenge. The others continue to linger in the halls of vague speculation.

Omnipresent God is omnipresent right action. In It you are immersed. In you, It says: "Go forward." It demands accomplishment. Knowing what you want and how to achieve it, you are an ally of the Divine. Thinking what you want and steadfastness in your self-discipline of mind makes you the delight of the Lord. The decided person is God's person. No power on earth can stop the one whose sights are set on goals and whose discipline is to that end. Others falter, but God's person moves up a step higher and proves their belief.

Your problem is your mountain to climb. God is with you. Divine Ideas guide you. Love enfolds you, and your thought causes the Law of Cause and Effect to establish you on the heights. Never rest in achievement. A goal secured is dangerous, for it is easy to be a success. Always, the Spirit impels you to a higher consciousness. God will never let you be a mediocre soul. God's Plan for you is far greater than your present mind can know. God's Wisdom sees all from the beginning to the never-ending conclusion.

The way to begin is to use spiritual mind treatment daily until you accomplish your present desire. Then, look out upon your vista of life and seek your next good. The universe cannot stop you. Its sole purpose is to cooperate. Start now on the second great goal you want. Believe that God wants you to have it. Pray effectively for its manifestation. Move up a notch, and then another. It is an endless pathway of glory.

We conquer mountains, and then seek higher ones to climb. This is a good technique for you. Keep your goals appearing. Never stop for an instant in your faith in right thinking. It is the answer to your problems. It is the movement of God through you. It is Life pressing upon you and bidding you follow the Highest. This is Religious Science.

THE WORLD NEEDS YOU

Back of the commonplace is always a touch of the Divine. As a Religious Scientist, you seek that inner Something in the everyday affairs of living. God is never isolated to a day, a time, or a ritual. The Infinite Mind is where you are, is what you are, and around you. It proclaims Its purpose. At hand is all the Goodness of the Spirit.

Life is the movement of a mighty Intelligence in action through Law. It produces for you whatever you select. God expects you to be as wise as God's Wisdom, so to you the Infinite gives of Itself without stint. It never commands you to greatness. It waits until you seek the greatness implanted in your consciousness from the beginning of time. The patience of the Almighty is tremendous.

Attempting to explain life in terms of birth, growth, maturity and death is futile. You can only understand yourself as a Spiritual activity when you view life from the heights of eternity. You know intuitively that your normal life span on earth cannot be all that you have been or will be. The God within whispers to you that there is an eternal plan and purpose. All religion has been to this end, and Religious Science emphasizes the Eternal Order of every living soul.

The positive, healthy mind moves forward according to the Divine Purpose. The confused, unhappy mind stagnates in its own infection. Jesus kept the faith of the right-minded vision. He beheld His God in every person and in every situation. He thought God, where others thought negatives. He loved with a Love Divine when those around Him argued and sought to satisfy their egos. His example excites those who seek a larger Path and a greater Outlook.

You can spiritually do more for the world than you think you can. The world at this time needs devoted people. It needs your consciousness of God, and your search for Spirit where you are. Your home, office, recreation and worship are all one thing. What you know of the nature of the Spirit within you acts in all places and attitudes. God appreciates your right thinking.

YOUR GREAT OPPORTUNITY

"Forgetting those things which are behind" is a part of the technique of Religious Science. These words of Paul are good therapy for spiritually-minded people. In our teaching we declare that you need not be the victim of the past. The total consciousness of the past year does not have to be a major influence of your life in the year to come.

Without spiritual understanding the past does continue to operate and govern the present, but this need not be so. Paul knew this and said "I die daily." It is a wise person who at the end of the day lets the problems of the day die, not carrying them through the night to awaken with them as still present. The continuity of your problems is dependent on you. The negatives of the past endure as long as you fail to behold yourself as God's present beloved activity.

God is not conditioned by the past. <u>God is always a Power of the now.</u> Infinite Mind never repeats an Idea. Life always progresses out of that which is known into that which will be. In you the Spirit is beckoning you forward. It is not interested in your tragedies, misfortunes nor hurts. It sees you as Its present outlet. It offers you all that the Infinite is, right now. Today is pregnant with God. This year is full of the immensity of what you can be.

If you want freedom this year, it is yours for the taking. If you want healing, peace, abundance or joy, God has provided these if you can change your patterns of thought to accept them. You do not depend upon God, but God's Mind depends upon you to bring to pass God's Ideas for you. Your receptivity is the important factor.

The forward look and the upward reach is the sign of spiritual unfoldment. Link your mind with that one great Mind and make this next year be what you want it to be. The blessing of God is upon you, and the respect of each person is given unto you. Let your Light so shine that all people will declare you blessed.

THE FAITH THAT DEMONSTRATES

Religious Science is a demonstrable religion. It never asks its students to merely accept its philosophy. It directs its followers to practice its premise, and prove for themselves the availability of the Divine Power. Upon the platform of works accomplished this worldwide ministry has been built. Its followers in ever-increasing numbers bear witness that our premise is true.

<u>Conviction is the basis of all spiritual techniques,</u> for without it no advancement can take place. Only as you move to larger ideas will your life have expanded experiences. Religious Science convinces you that you and the Creative Power are one process. Being one, you are the vehicle through which God acts at the point where you are.

As you convince yourself of your divine place in the grand overall process of Being, you begin to act as authority to your own experience. No longer does the world of opinions determine your thinking. You arise from the world thought and emerge as an original thinker in your own right. Only then can you be the person that God expects you to be.

In Truth all <u>people are equal</u>. <u>Great Ideas are available to you as much as to any other person.</u> The Infinite gives fully to all alike. Knowing your consciousness as a divine outlet of all that God is causes larger visions to come to your mind, healthier ideas to intrigue your imagination. It takes your thinking off where you are and places it on where you will be.

Convince yourself that you can demonstrate any good idea under the sun. <u>The world opinion will say you' can't, but the indwelling God whispers your capability</u>. Like Paul you can say "I can do all things through Christ which strengthened me." What others have done and are doing, you can do. If any person can be healed, you can be healed. If others prosper, you can prosper.

The breadth of your convictions of God as your Power determines the measure of your demonstration. Jesus had the full conviction of his unity with all Mind. What he accomplished is not at all amazing to the Religious Scientist. "Go thou and do likewise."

THE NECESSITY OF COURAGE

It takes courage to practice Religious Science. As Ideas of Truth infiltrate your thinking, you discover that old things, ideas and personalities must pass away in order that new forms of good shall appear. From the beginning of time, every advanced spiritual thinker has had to face themselves and decide if their spiritual understanding was great enough to meet this challenge.

The pathway of right thinking is straight, but the opportunities for detours are many. You may seek only self-gain and so bypass the central goal of spiritual unfoldment. Thousands of beginners in Religious Science are doing this. Fortunately, most of them come to their senses and discover that spiritual humility is greater than personal power.

If you really study this Science, it sets you apart. No longer are you interested in gossip, the negative news of the day or the wrong doings of others. Your eyes are set on a higher goal, and your mind and speech are dedicated to a more affirmative expression. Your loved ones, neighbors and business co-workers will not understand this. They will expect you to join them in their material thinking. Like the disciples of the Nazarene you will be misunderstood.

Jesus taught a way of life which demanded of his followers their strict adherence to spiritual truths, and their constant refutation of all that was unlike the Christ. Their courage to stand by Principle founded Christianity and made it a world force for good. You are in the same position. The world seeks a group of people who believe that sickness is nonsense, poverty means nothing, and frustration is unnecessary.

Every generation needs a new radical religious concept. We have it for this generation. Stand in your community as a true exponent of the New Thought of God and the larger Thought of Humanity. This will take courage, strength and a deep inner conviction that God is greater than evil. Doing this you are a pioneer for a new world religion.

Refute the necessity of disease, lack, inharmony and frustration. Declare audibly that you believe that Truth is omnipotent and Divine Mind is the only cause. Refuse to listen to evil in its many subtle forms. In this way, Religious Science will encircle the globe.

THE VITALITY OF CREATIVE THOUGHT

For ninety years[†] the doctrine of the power of thought has been preached to millions. This teaching preceded modern academic psychology and prepared the way for psychosomatic medicine. The Religious Science concept of thought processes differs from academic psychology, for it believes all thought to be spiritual.

The Emersonian concept of "One Mind common to all people," is the premise of our message. We believe that Jesus intuitively perceived a universal Mind in which all creation took place by means of thought. This was the source of his healing power, and he left a great teaching founded on this premise. He taught that belief determined experience.

No person ever made a more enlightening or freeing statement. That is why our civilization with all its human mind handicaps has steadily evolved and improved individual lives. It will continue to do so. Its progress will be speeded by movements such as ours which awaken millions to the recognition of the Mind of God as the only Cause and of each person as the thinking agent of that Mind.

Your thought is creative, because as you think the Creative Mind thinks as you. What you consistently think about must happen, for a Law of the Universe causes it to manifest. Jesus knew that his word had to become flesh. He relied on the creative Law of Mind to bring to pass what he selected should happen. To one

---

[†] *Editor's Note*: Barker is writing in the mid-1950s.

he gave healing, to another he gave peace of mind. His word could not return unto him void, for he knew that he was thinking into a Law which had to act as he directed It. You can do the same thing when you realize that your thought is Power, and the subconscious Law must produce it in form.

MIND IS YOUR SECURITY

The greatest search most people make is for security. Many readers of this book are still searching for it on the uncertain pathways of money, fame and success. Religious Science teaches an inner security based on a right understanding of your place in the Infinite Mind. Once you realize that God gives to you Ideas which are the starting place of all creative action, you seek these Ideas and accept them deep within your consciousness. You watch over them with right thinking and you trust them to deliver you forward in right action.

What you do with your mind is the most important action you take each day. If your thinking and feeling are fifty-one per cent positive, you are on the right road and you already have your security. You are wise enough to know that it does not come from the world. Security is an ==inner acceptance of yourself as victorious over negatives.== This you give to your world, and it must re-fashion itself to fit your premise.

Self-acceptance as God's creative person is your guarantee of favorable years to come. The universe never limits you, nor can other people's false ideas about the future confuse you. You can limit yourself and confuse yourself by believing the material lies. The longer you study Religious Science the more you handle life within your own consciousness by thinking rightly about it. You gladly assume the responsibility of your own security.

Jesus said he was in the world but not of it. He had a sense of correct values regarding his relationship to the world. Take this same attitude. All situations and conditions are extensions of your basic mental attitudes. Insecure people live in insecure worlds among insecure conditions. Jesus had an amazing inner security based on his knowledge of God, yet he lived in a very insecure material world. You can do likewise provided you keep your mental attitude constructive and you live with love and understanding.

Your basic security lies in the fact that the universe is primarily a mental system maintained by a Law of Mind. Where you are, you operate this Law. Jesus said that his teaching was the stone which the builders rejected. He taught a balanced mind in a healthy body with healthy emotional reactions sustained by a vision of each person as they really can be. That is your security in life.

MENTAL EFFICIENCY

Religious Science can simplify your life. It will remove the stresses and strains of modern living through your knowing God as the life you are living and the love you are releasing. A clear correct understanding of Infinite Mind and Its action as each person, removes all guilt from consciousness and permits streamlined thinking. It is a demonstrable science and anyone can prove the efficacy of its instruction.

God is Spirit. Spirit acts as Mind. Mind acts through Law. Each person receives spiritual ideas from the Universal Spirit. Our minds think them and subconsciously accept them. The subconscious of each person is their area of use in the Law. All ideas subconsciously accepted become manifest through the Law of God. This is the creative process which the Divine Intelligence devised and by which the experience of all people is determined.

A student of Religious Science is mentally efficient when they make certain that the only ideas they subconsciously accept are ones which they want to experience. Each person takes dominion over their world by controlling the ideas and emotions which saturate their consciousness. Knowing that thoughts create things, we handle thoughts with discretion and with purpose. We refuse to let our mind wander into bypaths of fear, resentment and discouragement. We hold our thinking to the line which we have set for ourselves, and we expect the Creative Process to make the demonstration for us, and It always does.

Moses knew what he wanted to accomplish and geared his thinking to that end. He did not let Pharaoh deter him from his goal. He thought what he wanted to experience and the Hebrew migration from slavery was the result. Jesus knew that God would honor his thought and act upon it. He thought God's health idea and the sick were healed through the Law of Mind. He knew plenty where others knew lack and proved the unlimited resources of the Divine Mind.

Negative ideas are as potent as positive ones. The Law produces either kind. It creates the kind of world you determine by your use of ideas. Place your thinking on as efficient a basis as you would your business or your home and have the desires of your heart. God never limits you. Stop limiting yourself.

A MODERN DEFINITION OF GOD

God is Infinite Intelligence, operating in an infinite field of emotion. All creation is in God and all creation is God, because there is only one Creative Intelligence creating out of Itself.

People modernize their homes, yet maintain in their modernized homes their same old thinking about God. We are modern on the outside and as old as time itself on the inside. We are living in a modern age, so why not be modern with our religion?

The metaphysicians were the first people to say that God is an unlimited infinite, creative Intelligence acting in a creative way, in all, through all and for all. Metaphysics has consistently proclaimed one immanent creative Power which in Its creation must act as Intelligence, and at the same time must act as a quality of feeling which the Bible has called Love. You think, but you also feel.

Whatever God is, It is something which acts at your level of thinking and feeling. It has to do this because there is no other place for It to act. An evolving person must have an evolving concept of God. With an expanding knowledge of ourselves and our universe, we are forced into an expanding understanding of God. Jesus announced that God and each person are one. Jesus announced one Creative Process and that each person individualized It. "He that seeth me seeth the One who sent me." (John 12:45) We are announcing this same truth in modern language. We say that the Infinite acts by means of the finite, and that the finite is the Infinite at the level of visibility or form. You are in God. God is in you. There is no separation, there never was and there never will be.

Every definition of God that you make today will be improved a year later. There is no such thing as a static God, any more than there is a static person or a static creation.

God is an ever-evolving Creative Process. You grow in It only as you allow yourself to grow with It.

THE FINGER OF GOD

In the depths of your consciousness is written the eternal words "This is my beloved child." The Finger of God has written it, and no person can destroy the heritage unlimited which forever awaits your recognition. The Infinite can never retract Its own statement. It can only know Itself as each person. It must ever love the fruits of Its own contemplation.

As you study Religious Science you seek the inner knowledge of your spiritual possibilities. You find this inner writing in your own soul. All books lead you to it. All teachers point the way. The pathway is through consciousness and not through dogmas. No outer person can give you your inner self-acceptance as God's own beloved. That is why the ancients called this teaching the "way of the lonely ones." It cannot be found in bunches, crowds or masses. The Infinite reveals Itself in the quiet mind and the open heart.

The first step on the pathway is right thinking based on right motives. The second is seeing your present world aright. The wise do not fight their experiences. They use them to prove the omnipresence of God. They resist not the material world; they function in it as directors. They find life well worth living, for they demonstrate the desires of their hearts. They know that no person can hurt them, rob them nor misdirect them. Their certainty is in the Spirit which they sense within themselves.

The third step in revealing the inner writing on your soul is practicing hourly the knowledge of Truth.

Every word becomes God-inspired. Every action becomes God-directed and every emotion releases the Love Divine. Doing this you sense that you are worthy of what the Finger of God has written in your inward consciousness. You rejoice in your full expression of the Infinite Mind. You understand the Law of life and your subconscious is cleared of all negatives. You know pure Cause and experience perfect Effect.

What God has written stands forever. You are the person God made after the pattern of God's Mind and flooded with the Love of God's Love. The three-fold pathway of blessedness is walked with ease as you sense the magnitude of the inner Spirit.

THE IMMEDIACY OF GOD

The idea of a personal God has intrigued humanity because thereby one could explain our own frailties. Only in the last few centuries has there been the expanded consciousness which affirmed a universal Creative Mind which caused all things to be. Gradually Omnipresence has taken hold in human thinking. Still to be universally accepted is the fact that God incarnates in each person as that person. This will be increasingly obvious as Religious Science expands its influence among millions.

The next idea for the human race to assimilate is that God only works in the instant. The Infinite is never conditioned by the past. It is a present force acting in present terms. God only knows what you are at the moment, and cannot judge you by your past. Psychology religions the past, Religious Science negates it.

The answer to every problem is in your knowledge of God and your ability to let Divine Ideas lead you to the correct solution. The healing action of Life is already in action, but you have to perceive that you are immersed in It. It requires your mental recognition in order to act in you and produce for you. It does not need to be beseeched, God merely requires calm acceptance as already being. By acknowledging a present God, unconditioned by your past and not fearing your future, the Power acts and the demonstration is made.

Create the Life You Want

To fear the future or to dwell in the past is to unconsciously limit the availability of God in your present experience. These are the false detours that many take. They lead to trouble, while knowing God at the moment leads to peace and plenty. The way out of the problems of today is not by means of either yesterday or tomorrow. The Power that already abides in you acts as you when you are clear in your thinking and uncluttered by emotional nonsense premised upon negations from former times. You can have what you want, but you have to think what you want, and you have to think of it as already being so. This is the science that Jesus exemplified.

WHERE ARE YOU GOING?

Your great desires lead you ahead. Your thinking follows your desires, and where your thinking goes, you go. Knowing this, Jesus taught a technique of belief. He knew that your destiny as a Spiritual Being was determined by the God that forever is. But, he also knew that few people would keep their desires geared to the good and their thinking in Heaven. So, he taught that you demonstrate your belief. Good, bad or indifferent, you demonstrate it.

There is no predestination in the Divine Plan, except for your ultimate good. You are a free agent in a Life which forever leaves you free to create what you want. The people who have been good, bad or indifferent have been people who consciously or unconsciously chose to be what they were. They went where their minds took them.

Religious Science has proved that sickness, lack, guilt and frustration have no reality. Every negative is curable through a spiritual method. The world does not make you sick, unhappy or poor. Your mind does. God is never interested in your problem. The Divine Mind has as Its only interest the solution. When you desire the answer to your problem, and think in its terms, you mind will deliver you to the solution. It is up to you whether Life deals the cards your way or not.

There is no chance, luck or good fortune in this world. All is law and order. Knowing this, you can arrange your desires and your thinking to produce what you want when you want it. Other religious bodies will say that you can't do this, but Religious Scientists do just this every day. They prove that the power of Mind is greater than any material force there may be. They demonstrate health, prosperity, happiness and peace of mind through a spiritual technique.

If you do not like the pathway your life seems to be heading, you can change it. The word impossibility was unknown to Jesus, Abraham, Moses, Isaiah and later great figures of Religion. To each of these God was an inner Presence whose Intelligence supported them in every right decision. This also applies to you.

THE DIVINE ECONOMY

The creative Spirit of living is mathematical in Its exactness. The Spirit acts through Mind, which in turn acts through Law. There is a Divine Precision which you can bring into your life. You do this by making your consciousness a precise instrument into which you pour only that which you want to experience. Wise people do not think in a hit or miss fashion. ==They know what they want and make certain that their desire dominates their consciousness.==

Your mind is the key to your experience, and your use of it determines your health, prosperity and security. To you God gave the greatest gift God could ever bestow. It is the gift of creative thought. The Infinite created you as Itself; and, as you think, the One Mind thinks by means of you. There is never a waste of thought or feeling. God is exact in Its operation, and there are no wastebaskets in the Divine Order. Everything produces after its own kind.

The Holy Spirit of creative thought is in all your thinking, not merely when you are thinking of the good. It is in your worry, your fear and your bitterness. That is why your troubles come upon you. The Divine Creativeness cannot be stilled. Mind is Its action, and your consciousness is Its distributor. To say one line of thinking is creative, and another is not is to fool yourself. The Divine Power is the constant action of your mentality, and with a complete precision it fashions your thought into form.

Knowing this, Jesus evidenced what a right-minded, God-centered individual could do. He thought in terms of what he wanted, and his word demonstrated results which are guideposts to greater living for all people. He knew that the Divine Economy was such that not a single thought or feeling could be spared for negatives. For three years he taught people to love Truth, think Truth and act the Truth.

To be economical in your use of negatives is a way to wisdom. You cannot afford the luxury of wrong thought. The price is too high and the results are too certain. Use your thinking to honor the Power which caused you to be.

THE AVAILABILITY OF WISDOM

The nature of the Divine is everywhere equally present. The Creator must indwell Its creation, and God must be in you. There is no vagueness about this indwelling Presence. It is Mind and It uses your mind as Its seat of operation. The nature of God is a Divine Givingness, and in you this Nature offers Itself without stint.

God as Mind in you offers you Its Ideas. These Ideas are persistently urging you to greatness. They seek to have you become the fullness and the whole stature of God. In your consciousness is the availability of God. You need not seek It afar, nor in an edifice. It is the inner urge to greatness. It is your intuition. The Spirit indwelling you thinks rightly of you.

Wisdom is the acceptance of a Divine Idea and the translation of that Idea into actual mental practice. The inspired have been many, but those who have made inspiration a fact in their experience have been few. There are no special favorites of God. God loves every person, and gives of Divinity equally to everyone. Those who sense the inner Wisdom and act upon it improve their lot. The others feel that God has passed them by.

Wisdom is not predicated upon education, although education may help you to understand Its processes and thereby manifest It with accuracy. Wisdom is the Divine Mind speaking in your mind as your mind. Religious Science believes in the divinity of every person. It believes that within you God is seeking to be all that God can be. Your awareness of this fact makes it possible.

As you affirm that Divine Wisdom is yours right here and right now, It acts in you as inspiration. It gives you Ideas you have never before known. They may startle you, and your first reaction may be that they are beyond your ability to demonstrate. God has always jolted us into greatness. Divine Mind is forever unique, and to all commonplace thinking Its Ideas are beyond acceptance.

Jesus accepted God as his source of wisdom. He acted upon the Ideas which arose in his consciousness. He did not doubt them. He knew they were true guidance in right directions. Follow him by doing the same.

EACH PERSON IS GOD'S REPRESENTATIVE

The word "represent" means to re-present, or to present again an idea which has previously been known, experienced or affirmed. Each person is a complete Idea in the Divine Mind, and by means of the Creative Process is representing this Idea in the world. Each destiny is great, and the fulfillment of each person is certain. As we evolve in spiritual understanding, we see ourselves aright, and accept the responsibility of bearing witness to the Truth.

It is evident that each person is not self-created, nor self-maintained. Behind us stands a mighty Mind in which all plans and purposes are known. This Mind sends us forth to be Its representative, and to act with authority in our environment, personal relationships and general affairs. To each of us is given a mentality, a field of emotions and an intuitive need for evolution. To each of us is also given the freedom to choose our own pathway and to regulate our own thinking.

Emerson said that our only sin was ignorance. By not realizing our Divine Purpose, we have detoured our mental causation into by-paths of strange selection. Knowing Religious Science, we return from our wanderings in the field of causation, and create that which is worthy of our high calling. We waste not at the level of cause and want not at the level of effect. Knowing the Truth each of us re-presents the Truth to the world.

To demonstrate this Science, you have to accept what God thinks of you, and not the opinions of others, nor your own wrong conclusions. The Infinite knows you as the individualization of Itself. Until you know this, you cannot represent the Mind which fashioned you out of Itself as the image and likeness of Itself. Once you are certain of your Divine Origin you assume a completely new role in living. You know that all situations are subject to your thought and conviction.

Then, you understand the meaning of "All power is given unto me in heaven and on earth." You become the Person God intended you to be, and you act with conviction in the creating of good for yourself and others.

I LIVE WITH EXPECTANCY

The student of this Science does not delay their good by believing in limitation. Each of us rises from the complacency of material thinking and asserts our divine prerogatives. Each acts with Divine Inspiration knowing that no negative is permanent and no problem is beyond solution. We expect our thoughts to be acted upon by the Law of Mind.

To live with expectancy is to live spiritually. Jesus expected God to be in every person, and God responded as healing. He was certain that Love was a balm for all ills, and by giving this Love he demonstrated Its virtue. His mind was God-centered and his actions were God-dominated. His example remains for all to witness and emulate.

Looking ahead ten years, what do you expect Life to deliver to your doorstep? Can you behold age and see it as a blessing? Can you look at the questionable economic facts of the current scene and know your prosperity is not dependent upon them? If you understand God as the center and circumference of your life, you can do this. This requires high vision and a faith that belies human appraisals.

The expectant mind accepts its good as certain, and does not question the steps involved in its fulfillment. This person's sight is set upon the goal, and nothing deters their imaging of the ideal. We affirm God as our certainty, and rest in the wise contemplation of our desire as fulfilled. We are not swayed by the opinions of others, nor by world reports by the highest authorities. We know the Truth of unlimitedness, and we gear our thinking to be expectancy of the good.

There is no permanent restriction in life. God is the door to a larger experience and this door remains forever open to your receptivity. On every hand the goodness of Life asks your acceptance. It bids you be rid of the petty, and acknowledge the great. Love leads you to fulfillment and Peace is known where you are. This is the practice of Religious Science.

To accept limitation is blasphemy. God knows it not, and as God's representative on earth you cannot afford it. The Infinite expects you to be great in your release of Life. Expect the impossible, for God knows it is possible.

THE INFINITE THINKER

Creation examined denotes a Creator which thinks with exactness and creates with precision. Religious Science emphasizes the Creative Process more than most religious systems. We do this for we realize that the universe is more of a process than it is a fact. It is an eternal arena of change for the manifestation of a Changeless Wisdom.

The world is still in process of creation; it will never be finished. The new will forever appear and the old will forever disappear. God as Mind is the eternal process of creating new Ideas by thinking new thoughts. Manifestation is the persistent interplay of new ideas versus old ideas. Inspiration is the inflow of the Creative Process in the minds of everyone. Desperation is the false attempt to maintain ideas after they have served their usefulness.

As you expand your knowledge of God as a Mind, forever thinking, forever creating Ideas, you are at peace in the midst of the ceaseless change, for you know its normalcy. As you expand your knowledge of God as the Law of the creative process, you realize the futility of maintaining any idea, situation or condition which has finished its course. What Mind conceives Law executes and no person can stop this eternal action which is forever making all things new.

The Infinite has planned a perfect universe and is doing all It can to cause its creation and its maintenance. We, in misusing our free will, have not cooperated, and our attempts to hold on to what is rather than seek that which shall be is the cause of all the error and disorder prevalent today, and in previous ages.

Religious Science seeks to give each person a correct knowledge of God and the way in which God works, thereby teaching us that the kingdom of heaven on earth is a present possibility, when we cooperate with God. As you think of God as the Infinite Presence in action, as the ideas of the Infinite Thinker reveal themselves in your consciousness, you are led out of the house of bondage-to-old-patterns, into the kingdom of God of new and greater experience.

THERE IS A GOODNESS

It has become fashionable to complain about everything. Grumbling is considered normal and anyone who is always cheerful is looked upon with suspicion. The errors of the world situation are emphasized and most people face the future with apprehension.

Religious Science proclaims the present world as good, and states that life, here and now, can be constructive. It teaches that God is always on our pathway and the future is bright with promise. It is a positive spiritual instruction. The practice of Religious Science assures any devotee of health, peace, prosperity and joy. It is not a Pollyanna system of escape from reality. Rather, it plunges the student into reality by explaining the nature of God and of humanity. It teaches a law of mind which can be directed by anyone.

Jesus told those who listened to him that heaven was where they were, and that good would always overcome evil. Religious Science believes this and proves it. Pessimism is the acceptance of evil as normal and necessary. True spiritual thinking denies this. The world, being impersonal, responds to either system of thought.

The Spirit in each person is never conditioned by their negation, but does spring forth into form through their affirmative thinking. God is still looking out upon the world and seeing it as good. God is still thinking of us as His image and likeness. There will always be right-minded people to keep the Light shining, and we are among them. There is always more good than evil, and we are the seekers of the good.

God's action is always instant. Where the forces of evil seem to prevail, the omnipresence of the Infinite Goodness is offering Itself. Those who seek the Light find Omnipresence in action. Those who hold to the falsities of human reasoning believe that the Light has ceased. God will never go out of business, and in the long run human pessimism must fail.

The world is the arena of God's possibility, and each of us is the vehicle of exploration. Everything is for us and nothing is opposed to our heart's desires. The abundant life promised of old is as near as your positive thinking.

WATCH YOUR MIND

Anyone who takes as much interest in the trends of their thinking as they do in the way they spends their money, can demonstrate Religious Science and have its benefits. Religious Science is a science of the mind. It reveals Mind as cause, and points out the true value of affirmatives and the destructive action of negatives. It is religious because it teaches that God acts in each person as Mind. It is scientific because it has a definite law of action, and can offer proven results.

Where your thinking goes, your affairs follow. Life is complex and hard for all who run around in mental circles, seeking to manipulate conditions with more conditions. In the unnecessary maze of mental contradictions, they believe that life is against them, and God has willed their troubles. Such people scoff at the possibility of Religious Science helping them. They want a religion which justifies their problems, instead of one which solves them.

Life becomes simplified and successful when you leave the maze of mental confusion and start the discipline of right thinking. Your mind is the beginning and the end of your difficulties. It is also the beginning and the end of your successful living. God is impersonal and leaves you free to go either pathway. Ideas are the greatest potential for good or evil there is or ever will be. Creative Ideas allowed to have dominance in your mind will bring forth rich treasures of ease, health and love.

All of God is where you are at every instant. A correct knowledge of God produces right thinking about yourself, others and the world in which you live. Declare that God surrounds you and in-dwells you as Spirit, Mind and Love. Then, gear all your thinking for twenty-four hours to that basis. Watch the way your thinking goes and check it each time a negative seeks to control. Watch your reactions to others and be certain you think rightly about them. This proven technique works, and you can work it.

Gradually, such thinking will destroy the negative patterns of a lifetime, and bring forth new mental and emotional patterns that are worthy of the Divinity which did create you and which forever indwells you.

THE DIRECTED MIND

Thought controlled is experience determined. Life requires of us disciplined thinking, if we are to become the full expressions of God's plan. We can tarry in the halls of hope, dream and vision. Or, we can do something this day to bring to pass the desires of our hearts. The Infinite Mind never inhibits our freedom. We stand in the limitless possibility of greatness, or the limitless possibility of failure. In our consciousness alone we determine our lives and their results.

The world does not believe this. Most people live undirected lives and experience both good and evil. The Religious Scientist assumes the responsibility of living. We know that God has made us for a purpose and left us free to create our own good from the limitless Ideas that Divine Mind offers to us. We open our thinking to greatness through treatment, and live in the constant expectancy that God does honor God's thought and does act upon it.

Through Religious Science the sick are healed, the poverty thinker is prospered and the unhappy are made glad. This is accomplished because God operates in each us as us. We determine our own destinies. We decide either consciously or unconsciously what shall come to pass in our individual worlds. Upon our shoulders rests the importance of decision. We declare the Ideas of God to be ours. We think them with deliberate certainty. We know that the Law of Mind causes them to materialize in form. We rest in a sure method of demonstration. By our works we are known.

"Choose ye this day whom ye will serve." Evil is fascinating and easily claims the attention of the undedicated mind. Good need not be delayed if your thought is clear and your purpose is right. Your good is at hand. God wants you to be successful. Think seriously of the good you have. Then, think of the greater good that you can have, and declare that it is coming to pass. God will not fail you, if you do not fail yourself.

MIND INSPIRES EACH OF US

The Infinite wants you to bring to pass the desires of your heart. It offers you Its great Ideas and leaves you free to bring them to accomplishment. Whether you do this or not is up to you. Millions have been inspired, but only a few hundreds have really done things. Ideas are as free as the air you breathe. But, accept them you must, and act upon them you must, if your better experience is to be a fact.

Your use of ideas determines your experience. This always has been so, and is so now. The Great have achieved greatness because they took their inspiration and added to it their perspiration. Ideas without a means of production in form are useless. To be inspired is the action of God in us. To produce results is our responsibility.

You cannot shirk this responsibility. Excuses are delay. The eternal Spirit tolerates them only for a time. In each of us God planted greatness, for "in the image and likeness of God made He them." Mind expects you to demonstrate your good. In the long run of eternity, It demands that you do it. God expects the highest and best of each of God's creations.

Ideas happen to you, so use them. God is inspiring you every moment of your day. God's Presence surrounds you, and God's Mind acts in you. Your subconscious is waiting for you to plant in it ideas that will create the greatness you seek.

Say to yourself, "I now subconsciously accept Divine Ideas: I give them to the subconscious Law of

Mind. I know that this Law is now in action bringing them to fruition. I rejoice that by my acceptance of my good it is already established unto me. I rest in the sure knowledge that God as Law will bring it to pass. This is so right here and right now."

Then, expect your good to take place. Think in terms of its happening. Refute all evil and affirm all good. This is the essence of Religious Science. Watch your trends of thinking, and make certain that they are toward your goal. You are the only factor which can ruin your demonstration. Others do not influence you, and the world has no power to limit you.

God wants you to have the good and great things you want. God's Mind upholds you as you discipline yourself to bring these to actual form.

YOU ARE A FREE AGENT

The law of life is one of freedom. It has no power nor authority within Itself to limit you. Your limitations are unconsciously self-accepted. But, with knowledge of Religious Science you can break through any barrier. You can prove that the power of God-thinking will heal your body, prosper your affairs, and maintain pleasant personal relationships. Millions have proven this fact.

Jesus was never limited by the conditions of the world around him. He proved that thinking in terms of God delivered you from the conditions created by those who thought in terms of limitation. Because disease was not a part of his thinking, he could heal those who had accepted it. He knew that every person was free, if only they would seek God within, and think in God's terms.

You are free, because you are cause to your world. What you think causes an experience to happen. Being free to think anything you wish, you can cause either good or trouble. No one thinks in your mind but yourself. No other person can think for you. You are the sole originating cause of your experience. Knowing this, you no longer blame the world or other people for the evil that befalls you.

The Garden of Eden is still where you are, but your eyes no longer behold it, for your thinking is conditioned by your years of meeting situations. Eating of the tree of good and evil in your thinking, you create both for yourself. Without realizing it, you expel yourself from your good. The world owes you nothing, for it can only give back to you what you cause in your mind.

You are cause and the world is effect. You are action and the material experience in which you are functioning is reaction. You are a Creative Thinker in a Law which acts upon your thought and brings to pass an experience like unto it. Jesus thought God and experienced God. He knew that he was the creator of his own experience, and therefore, he projected what he wanted. He demonstrated health, money, peace, love, harmonious relationships with others, and gave the world truths which have permanently improved it. You can do likewise.

THE SUPREME STATEMENT OF LIFE

"I and my Father are One." The world has improved because a positive man stood in a negative environment and uttered these words. His statement was true. He knew its Truth and with conviction declared It as his basis. It changed history. If you will speak it with a similar conviction, it will change your life. These words are the summation of all Truth. They announce that God and each person are one process.

God, the One Mind, forever expresses as each person. You are God at the level of visibility. You are all that God is and has. You don't really believe this, but it is so. Jesus believed it, and was able to demonstrate the Truth of this statement. Too long have you thought of yourself as a sinner. Too little have you known yourself as a saint. But, the saint is what you are, the sinner is merely what you have believed about yourself.

A positive idea always destroys a negative condition. Knowing this, Jesus proved the divinity of every person. He announced a positive idea of life. It healed, resurrected, prospered and enriched all whom he encountered. He knew what he was, where he was going and unlimited power he had to disperse. He acted and the world around him reacted. One man knowing Truth healed hundreds who as yet had not known Truth.

How much of each day are you declaring positives? You are one with God, and your word has power. Act as God to your world and you will behold the problems crumble before your word. Nothing can stop the progressing forward action of someone who knows they are a Spiritual Power in a world which must become what their word affirms. Stand at a point of authority and command your experience.

As long as you think of yourself as a human being, you will struggle to bring forth success. All Mind is yours to use. All Power seeks you as Its outlet. All Love offers Itself to you for dispersal. Conceive of yourself as Divine, and then act as a Spiritual being. Be what you ought to be.

THE NEW IS APPEARING

Static ideas maintain present ·conditions, but creative ideas cause new things to appear. You can stay as you are by thinking what you usually think. Or, you can fulfill your spiritual destiny and let new ideas appear by means of you. Divine Inspiration has never been depleted and you can tap It right where you are.

Inspiration is never limited to any person or group. Being of God, It flows through the mind which welcomes It. You avail yourself of It by believing that It is in action right now in your mind. It requires neither fasting, adherence to a particular religion, nor vain imploring. God as Mind is already the center of your thinking. It bids you to expect new ideas, greater than any that you have ever known before.

Spring is the emergence of new forms of life and beauty. They arise from the seeming latent ground of winter. Yet, below the ground an Infinite Intelligence has been active preparing all that was necessary for their appearing. In the depths of your soul are Divine Ideas preparing to come forth by means of your mental acceptance and cooperation. God has done God's part. God expects you to do yours.

Your whole being craves the new. It knows and has finished its work with the already experienced situations. It needs new forms of life, abundance, love and goodness. Affirm that the newness and freshness of Spring appear in your mind as well as in your world. Seek the different, for in it is the key to creative imagination. From within your own mind bring out new interests, develop new friends, do new things.

Dull people stay as they are. Spiritually alert people keep ahead of the times. Readers of this book know that causation begins when you declare your mind open to the Universal Spirit and watch for Its Ideas to appear. New ideas in consciousness guarantee new conditions in your experience.

Say to yourself: "I know that God is at the center of my being. God's Mind inspires me. God's Love quickens me. In all ways I am made new. There is now appearing greater good for me, and I accept it with joy."

THE POWER TO ACCOMPLISH

Unto you is given the power to create and accomplish in life the deep desires of your heart. The incarnation of God in you, as you, is this power. Freely It is given to all alike. Some intuitively realize this and bring forth great works. Others are lulled by their material acceptances from childhood to the present and never realize that within them is this unconditioned possibility.

The Infinite expects the finite to reproduce in its area all that which the Infinite is. God's expectation is upon you. It bids you arise from the lethargy of what you believe, and move into the area of sure knowledge, which is spiritual. You may believe you cannot succeed, but God expects you to prosper and has equipped you to do so. You may believe that the world is against you, but the Divine knows that in your inward parts is written a right use of the Law of Mind which can change the world.

The Power of God to accomplish does not ask for your supplication. It awaits your recognition that It is. As you act with authority, the Power accepts your direction and brings to pass your dictates. Piety and meekness limit the free action of God. Sincerity and intention give It freedom to perform Its full mission. The determined mind is the divinely operating mind. Indecision and dependence upon the opinions of others withhold the good you can have. Only you and God know what is right action for you. Even the one closest to you cannot know this secret between you and your Maker.

"Arise, shine, for thy light is come," was Isaiah's way of telling us to start living life fully and getting from it the rewards of our right thinking. Take one goal you seek. Declare that it is Spiritual and Divine. Affirm that the Law of Mind is now bringing this goal to pass. Do this several times each day for thirty days.

Never once let your mind speculate upon the possibility of not achieving your desire. Hold your thinking to the line of expectancy. Your daily treatments, plus the watching of your consciousness to prevent negation, will give the Law freedom to act. You will be amazed at the result.

YOU NEED A SPIRITUAL BASIS

Materially-minded people miss a great deal in life. They don't believe this, for they are busy with "things" and accomplishments. But, the ends they seek and the means they use exhaust them. They weary early in years and decline with rapidity. They seem to need self-fulfillment.

The spiritually-minded person accomplishes with ease, health and peace of mind. Their way is less troubled and their energy is less exhausted. You can select either path. You can "labor with the sweat of your brow" as did Adam, or accomplish with the ease of Christ. God leaves you free, and the universe responds to you no matter which path you select.

God seeks to give birth to God's ideas in your mind. You are God's point of conception. You are always the mother of your world, when you live the life of the Spirit. As you welcome the indwelling God in your mind, God's inspiration gives birth to great ideas. These lift you from your present level to a higher one. They raise you from the stratum of material manipulation to the level of calm acceptance.

"My yoke is easy and my burden is light." The God-directed mind knows the truth of this statement. Your attention on Spirit releases your attention from negatives. Their enthrallment passes, and the good seeks you out. Life wants you to have the best, the finest and the true. It offers you Itself. It beckons you toward greatness.

Create the Life You Want

The more you affirm that God is your life, the greater efficiency you will have for effectual expression. Our active acknowledgment of the Truth clears the cob-webs from our thinking and clarifies our conclusions. Power increases, fatigue lessens and we accomplish with ease.

Be a God-premised individual. "Underneath are the everlasting arms." This is Divine Security. This is the path of faith which you walk with your attention forward and your world responds in manifesting the glory of God. Your mind is linked with all who have known God as their fortress. You joined the ranks of the mighty who let God be in them all that God can be.

The years to come are pregnant with good. Those with uncluttered minds shall have this good, for without fear Faith appears. The Christ in you leads you from glory to glory.

THE ATTITUDE WHIC[H...]

The inquiring mind asks why som[e ...] others do not. On the surface, it would seem that many who have no spiritual insight or interest live in plenty, while others with great religious convictions live in want. Your study of Religious Science will straighten out your thinking on this question, and give you the key to greater financial ease in your world.

Consciousness is the determining factor, and the Law of Mind does not know whether the individual using It is spiritually-minded or not. One of the questions raised in the Book of Psalms was "Why do the wicked flourish?" They flourish because they know what they want, think in its terms, and refuse to believe that it is impossible to have it.

What you want, and what you think are quite often two different things. We can all learn a lesson from unprincipled people. They use the same Law of Mind as we use. But, they use It with definite intention. They are certain of where they are going, and how they will achieve their ends. Are you certain of where you are going, and are you clear on how to achieve the goals you have hoped to achieve?

"Unto everyone which hath shall be given and from those that hath not, even what they hath shall be taken away from them." (Luke 19:26) Jesus taught a Law of consciousness. He knew why the wicked flourished and why most "good" people did not. He sought to make virtuous people as radical in their affirmative

...ing and speaking as the unprincipled are in ...eirs. He taught the Law of Mind and practiced It.

Where your consciousness leads, your affairs follow. People in financial problems do not talk abundance. Sick people do not discuss health. Unhappy people do not affirm joy. If they did, their problems would be solved.

To those who have a prosperity consciousness, ever-increasing plenty comes. It comes because the Law takes what these people give It and demonstrates It. The poor get poorer and the rich get richer, because Life acts through Law.

Knowing this, you can do something about it. Take Jesus' statement to heart. Use the idea deliberately. This is the practice of Religious Science.

THE RIGHT-MINDED PROSPER

God respects and cooperates with God's creations. The Mind which originated us planned its functioning in ease, health and love. The Divine Principle has never failed to do Its part. It has always responded when a call has been made upon It.

You can be right-minded and experience the goodness of Life, or you can follow the dictates of your own opinions and take the results of your own mistakes. The Bible declares our freedom to create heaven or hell. You have probably had a mixture of both.

Inspiration is the conscious action of God in us suggesting that we be right-minded. It leads to the expansion of our faculties, and our larger use of them for constructive purposes. It assures you that your individual good is backed up by the universal Good which God is. Isolation and loneliness are spiritual impossibilities. God can never know your self-will, nor ever be aware of you as separate from Itself. It forever re-creates Its creation and enfolds it in Its own beneficent Presence.

The person who enriches their mind with spiritual ideas will prosper. Their health will be assured, and their capacity to give and receive love will be active. Their fears will be minor and their achievements effortless, for their consciousness knows its inner spiritual ability to meet life in all right ways.

Religious Scientists use daily treatments to keep alive the spiritual foundations of their natures. It is not easy to keep the thinking geared to Truth. No messiah, prophet nor savior found it easy either. It is only definite daily practice of positive ideas which brings ease and peace.

You can demonstrate in your life what you choose. This is the teaching of Jesus, and other great leaders of spiritual thinking. Religious Science Churches, groups and literature give you the technique. A scientist, however, having learned a technique proceeds to apply it to a specific problem. Take the Law of Mind as you now know it and apply it to your problem. God supports you as you do this, for God's Mind must respond to your right-mindedness.

THE DETERMINING FACTOR OF THOUGHT

You are the Divine possibility. You are never an isolated creation. You are an integral part of the Infinite Process and the Infinite Plan.

Not knowing this, humanity seeks only its own gain. People fight for their supposed rights, cheat one another, and hang millstones about their own necks. This book is designed to awaken you to the knowledge that such is not necessary to live abundantly. Religious Science believes in you, because it first believes in a universal Spirit, from which you sprang.

Spirit is the universal creative power; Mind is the way It works, and each of us is the means of Its full expression. You do not yet realize all that you can be. The world of form ensnares you in its hypnotic false opinions. Power, money and ease are the modern goals. Yet, every Messiah has taught the opposite.

Jesus said "In the world ye shall have tribulation: but be of good cheer, I have overcome the world." (John 16:33) This is your pathway. Cease the manipulation of matter, and begin the manipulation of ideas. Power is in your mind and you are the thinker. Spirit infuses you with all that God is. Mind is your tool, and form is your area of reaction.

Your body cannot make you sick. It has neither power nor authority. It is a field of reaction, not of cause. It takes the imprint of your thought and acts upon it. It cannot do otherwise, for it is effect only.
God is Spirit, each of us is Spirit directing its execution in our world. Assume your birthright, and

act as a director of the Divine Stream of Life. Your mind action determines your world action. God in you, as you, thinks through you. When you think, God thinks. That is why your thought has power. Knowing that God as Spirit is Mind in action, you can think rightly and achieve greatly.

Select your major ideas with care. They will shortly appear in your world as concrete facts. Think constantly of God as your health, peace, security, prosperity and love. These will happen to you, because they are caused by you.

A YEAR OF GREATNESS

A new year inspires you to greatness. You look ahead and see the solution of your problems. You greet it with hope, vision and optimism. This is exactly what Religious Science teaches. But, to hold that vision steadfastly through twelve long months is almost impossible for anyone. Even in late January most people have returned to their unconscious acceptance of defeat. They fail to keep the high standard of right thinking. The readers of this book can prove for all the world to see that any hope sustained consistently becomes a fact in actual experience.

The mind of Jesus expected God to deliver through Law the ideas that he nourished. He never accepted defeat. He never anticipated failure. He kept his thinking hewed to the line of great ideas, and his demonstrations two thousand years ago changed the course of history. As Orthodoxy developed his essential message was lost in ritual and symbolism, but in each age there have been those who kept the lantern of his true teachings alive. Religious Science does this for this age.

One year from this day you will either be exactly as you are, or you will be an improved person. Your thought, and your thought alone, determines which you will be. No person can make you a saint, and no person can make you a sinner. You stand always in the atmosphere of your own consciousness and experience the result of your own contemplations. The divine Law of justice rules and governs your life. There is no one to blame and there is no power that creates miracles. God is Order through Law. God's Love leads you to greatness, but God's Law delivers to you your own just deserts.

A new year brings promise to those who can change their consciousness through disciplined thinking and feeling. To the rest it brings repetition. Take your highest visions, hopes and desires and believe them true. Think in terms of them, and know that the Infinite wants you to experience them. There is no power opposed to your creative thinking. Twelve months of greatness greet you with their potentials, or, one month of hope and eleven of unconscious acceptance of the usual troubles.

Religious Scientists accept in the now what they know will happen in the future. Like Jesus they believe that all things are possible to a clear mind in a healthy emotional arena.

THE VICTORY OF EASTER

There is a divine power resident in every person which resurrects them from the problems of living. Jesus gave evidence of this power and told his followers to follow him in the use of it. Within you this power claims your attention. It beckons you to accomplish greatly and not be defeated. There will always be a stone on your pathway which must be rolled away, but the power of God in you will accomplish this.

Easter offers the opportunity to emerge from the problems of the present into greater freedom in the immediate future. No tomb of material problems can stop the individual who knows God as their true self, and directs their mind aright. Resurrection is the action of God in us bringing God forth from the tomb of our own errors of omission and commission.

Jesus exemplified the spiritual person and the spiritual person's ability to overcome the problems of this world. On Easter morning Jesus proved that Life is indestructible and Love forever reigns. You are deathless, immortal and free. Within you on your pathway is the power to meet all that comes. You may be tried in the balances, but leaning on the inner Mind you will not be found wanting. Remember, Jesus was only three hours on the cross and that is as long as any difficulty should enslave you.

With the inner power to resurrect your life comes the Glory of Easter. Its beauty, freshness and drama portray the victory you have found within. Jesus maintained his thinking in heaven, while his feet trod the paths of human experience. Follow that pattern and you will emerge from defeat to victory. Dedicate your thinking this month not to the cross of your problem, but to the open tomb of your freedom. Thinking in terms of your problem nails you more firmly to the cross. Thinking in terms of God's solution of your trouble delivers you into a larger life and a greater experience.

The old patterns, the unworthy thoughts need to be crossed out of mind. They deserve their crucifixion. God bids you to be resurrected into a larger area of life. The stone rolls away as you know Truth, love Truth and appreciate Truth. With Easter in your mind, there will be glory in your world.

BE THANKFUL

Glad is the person who sees life as a spiritual experience to be lived with wisdom and from which joy can be reaped. Their heart rejoices. Their work is easy and their burden is light. Cold science with its accuracy does not evoke gratitude to the laws which it has found. In Religious Science, we praise and appreciate the Infinite Mind which acts as Law but is also the presence of Love.

We see life as the action of God, an action which frees us to our own experience. Law does not limit us. Our right use of thought and feeling makes the Law beneficent. Our wrong use of It makes us Its slave to negatives. But, our freedom to change from enslavement-to-circumstances to emancipation from circumstances is our eternal heritage. For this we give thanks, rejoice and are glad.

We should praise our freedom to create the good, negate the evil and bring to pass the desires of our hearts. Our attention should be on those things which can be and not on why we have achieved so little when so much is available. Religious Science teaches the forward look and the creative value of the spiritual use of the imagination.

All bondage is temporary, whether it be disease, lack of money, disharmony in the home or unpleasant personal relationships. A corrected and redirected consciousness will always bring to pass a corrected situation. This is the law of redirected belief which Jesus explained to his followers. If disease were a permanent evil, he could never have healed it. Knowing its temporary nature, he could dismiss it with his clear thinking of its opposite.

Jesus gave thanks to the Power which healed. He saw thanksgiving as a necessary attitude to produce the best results in life. He knew that his belief acted as a Law, yet he also knew that the Power which caused his belief was greater than he was. We should praise the Spirit, the Mind, the Law and the Love of God. Give thanks for God, and for yourself in God as Its means of expression.

THE REAL MEANING OF CHRISTMAS

The divine economy knows when to lift the hearts of people. For each stage of evolution it announces Itself by means of a wise soul who will transmit the ideas to the multitudes. Christmas is the symbol of a Divine Revelation of God in us as us. A child symbolizes the fully matured adult. The manger reminds us of the simplicity of our own inner natures.

The Divine Witness of every person drew the attention of the wise men. Wisdom flows to the level of the awakened soul. The silent shepherds break into song as they behold their own greatness. Sing the song triumphant and you also will say that there is Glory to the Highest concept of God and there is order in all human relations. Peace is the automatic result of knowing God aright. In the quietness of spiritual understanding the knowledge of your relationship to the Universal is born.

God reveals God's Idea of our greatness as God's individualization. God proves that sin, sickness, poverty and death are not real. God announces for all times to come that Christ in us is victorious over the world's beliefs. Christmas is the knowing that Love permeates all, and Truth is the only common denominator. It is God's declaration of our emancipation from all limitation. The Infinite Mind asserts its own domination of creation. It refutes our attempts to glorify ourselves, by glorifying the person God created.

Create the Life You Want

In simplicity Divinity is born. Away from the crowd of human opinions Divine Ideas emerge to lift us from our belief in the reality of evil unto the Truth that evil is nothing. Like Mary of olden times, you can bring forth your first born, your new concept of yourself. You can assume the role of Divinity with which the Infinite has endowed you. You can become the Power which bids the waves of human wrong thinking to be still.

The Christ in you is God's release of His full nature. It is the eternal Christmas. It gives you the fullness and the richness of the Kingdom. Every gift salutes the God person you are. Every Christmas tree witnesses your ability to grow tall in the ways of Truth. God is forever blessing and benefiting God's own beloved -- you.

LIFE AS A CREATIVE EXPERIMENT

Few people think of life as a creative experiment. Most of us are so busy with routines that we take life for granted. We expect an endless routine of work, a hectic social life each weekend and two weeks' vacation each year. I trust that the readers of this book will derive from it a new interest in life, a zest for doing what needs to be done and a technique to live with joyous enthusiasm.

Looking at life from an inspired viewpoint you can see those things which are on the side of greatness and cease resisting the petty and the unimportant. Life is a process of intelligence. It always acts intelligently. Problems are the result of living life unintelligently.

Work with your world the way it works. To drive a car, you have to drive it the way a car should be driven. You can't drive it as you would a locomotive, an airplane or a boat. Life can be lived fully, provided you live it according to the basic patterns of Life itself.

The creative power in life is mind. That is its primary quality and its most basic function. The universe is the result of a mathematical thinker, thinking mathematically. One authority said that the only real difference between matter and mind was that mind is an area of ideas in fluidic form and matter is an area of ideas temporarily locked up in form.

The universe is actually a mental system. Its primary nature is the process of ideas becoming form. Every fact in your world is also an idea in your mind. To get new things in your world you must have new ideas in your consciousness. Few people do enough abstract thinking to create new ideas in their minds. They continually think about what they already know and have known for years. This explains the monotony of their lives.

To increase the area of humanity's consciousness has been the aim of all religion and education. The infiltration of new ideas in the mind is essential to healthy living. You exist in an infinite Mind which offers you an ever-expanding variety of ideas. Ideas are seeking to be born in your mind.

Select the idea of some new experience you want and then think it without ceasing. Mind will deliver to you everything you need in order to accomplish your demonstration. This is far from being impossible. The great, the wise and the true have proven this to be so. You have done it and so have your friends. You may not have thought of the process as being either spiritual or psychological. You intuitively knew a new idea. Your thinking in terms of this idea caused something to happen in your experience.

THE NECESSITY OF CREATIVE IDEAS

Power is not in what you do, what you own, nor in the health of your body. Power is in the use of your mind and emotions. Your consciousness determines the way life works for you, for it can only work for you by working through you. Ideas have to use the materials which are within you. These materials are your mental attitudes, your fears, your memory and your desires.

Ever since humanity began its first primitive groping for a belief in God, and thereby developed religion, our spiritual thinking has revealed to us one central idea. Every religion has taught it and every savior has exemplified it. It is that belief determines your experience. What you are on the inside determines what you experience on the outside. Your faith in good increases your area of good. Your faith in negatives, which is fear, increases your problems.

There is a science of the mind, a way of handling thought and feeling to get the most out of life. This science does not teach that you can be happy, prosperous and healthy all the time. That would be nonsense. However, this science does teach that you can greatly improve your mental attitudes and as a result you will certainly be happier, healthier and have greater ease in finance. These areas of life are determined by the types of ideas functioning in your consciousness, and you can always improve your ways of thinking and feeling.

Spiritual thinkers have realized the importance of directing the mind to great ideas rather than keeping it at the level of daily routines which absorb you with the petty, the tiresome and the disconcerting. Their advice has been to think of the nature of God, the living spirit within you and of those elements of life which are creative, expanding and eternal. If you have done this you have proven to yourself that this technique works. Fixing your attention on a positive goal causes Life to back you up with all its processes and you realize that the universe is for you and never against you. You live with greater ease and are able to give ease to others.

The Infinite Mind created your consciousness to be a positive, creative, active area of influence. Fears, unhappiness, sickness and lack are a misuse of your mind. It was never designed to work with these vicious and destructive emotions. That is why they wreak their havoc upon you. God knew what God was doing when God gave us the capacity to think in large terms, to perceive great truths and to experience love in its highest forms. You are divinely equipped to think what the great have thought, through their books, music, art, theatre and science. In addition, your equipment of consciousness includes your ability to have original ideas arise within you.

No person has ever contemplated their Divine Nature and not been benefited. From within comes the urge to select in life that which is greater than you now know. From this same intuitive source comes the whisper of God saying you need not be sick, unhappy, frustrated and struggling with financial problems. Life is an inlet and an outlet, an ebb and a flow. It is something you receive and give. Ideas enter your mind and actions follow. Thoughts come to your mind and you do something about them. If they are negative you worry, fear and doubt. If they are creative, you are inspired to right and loving action.

The Necessity of Creative Ideas

You are forever immersed in and a part of a Creative Mind. This Mind is thinking new ideas into your consciousness. Accept them by knowing that they come to you in order to operate through you and bring to pass something greater in your experience than you have had previously. Welcome them as you would a dear friend. Life seeks in every way to inspire your mind. It wants you to have more and more of all good things. It knows no lack, limitation nor impossibility. God never knows defeat.

There is no virtue in pain, poverty or unhappiness. Unhappiness has never improved a living soul. It cannot increase your area of good, it will only diminish it. It warps, destroys and contracts. The Infinite can only release Its ideas into the consciousness that is at peace with itself and enjoying the experience of living.

Happiness is determined by the ideas working in your consciousness, not by your environment, possessions, social activities or your hopes. Happiness knows no time, it is always a present action. Your mentality is always under your personal control. Your mind always displays itself. It makes itself obvious. As you enter a room people glance at you and know your mood. You give to others only what you are. In my book *Treat Yourself to Life* is this sentence: "Your happiness is in direct ratio to your ability to give yourself to others."

Givingness is the basis of all living. It is the cause of all friendship, love, family life and social activities. However, the boundaries of your mind determine your capacity to give. The ideas that predominate in your thinking are what you share with your world. Greatness offers itself to you. All of love gives of itself in you.

Life has never imprisoned anyone. It cannot, by its own nature, limit you. God offers to you Ideas which will make you free from the false conclusions of your own negative thinking. Take them and rejoice.

You are free to take what you want from life and give what you will to life. You are spiritually free, though for the moment you may be materially in bondage. Lack of income may, for the moment, prevent you from doing what you want.

Poor health, a sense of duty to family or an obligation to business is a passing experience to those who let in the ideas of God. You are free to think anything you want to think.

If you want to treat yourself to life, place your attention on ideas which will cause you to move ahead. These ideas already dwell in you and await your recognition. God in the midst of you is inspiring you at this moment. Say to yourself:

There is but one mind, one life, one good, God. To me are given the ideas of God, and they now are alive within me. I accept them with joy. I give them their full freedom to operate through me and bring to pass a finer experience for me. I give them all power and authority to accomplish their purpose. I rejoice in them and am glad.

The consistent repetition of ideas is a process of learning. Think back to your school days and you will verify this. In the field of mental attitudes the repetition of ideas is most important. The constant repetition of negatives in your thinking causes your subconscious mind to produce more difficulties in your experience. Possibly you dread the future. You can't see much health, prosperity or happiness ahead of you. If you will watch your thinking and your moods, you will discover the reason for this. Over the past months,

The Necessity of Creative Ideas

perhaps years, you have been mentally convincing yourself each day that the future is dark. From early morning until late at night, without realizing it, you consistently think and speak negatives. Your whole approach to your work and your recreation is the expectancy of trouble. Why wouldn't you feel depressed and be certain that others who are successful have a special claim on heaven.

The Bible teaches that your real inner thinking about yourself becomes a law to your experience. Such teaching is as old as the first wise person who ever lived and appreciated life. The repetition of trouble at the conscious mind level day after day indicates increased trouble ahead. Your religion should have taught you to believe in the goodness of life, its endless opportunities and your ability to achieve what you want, for the living Spirit indwells you.

If you are unhappy or in some form of tragedy, you may not believe this, but when you do believe it, your problems will begin their dissolution. Why should life give you anything better than what you now have, if your thinking remains at a dead level? A chronic invalid cannot gain health while their mental attitude maintains the illness. If you are in a chronic financial problem, why should the creative power prosper you, if your constant attention is on how little you have? Life can only give you what you are mentally conditioned to accept. Consistent belief that you haven't what you want will never cause what you want to happen to you.

There is an exactness to life; there is a science of living. The Creative Mind delivers to you the exact results of your states of mind. This is the law of cause and effect. Both Jesus and Paul taught it. You can only have in your world what you are mentally and emotionally conditioned to have. By changing your conditioning through the repetition of spiritual ideas, you change what you receive from life.

The power and wisdom of God have never planned a negative program for anyone. If you dread something in the future, you need a good swift spiritual shot in the arm. You need to treat yourself by contemplating the nature of God and your place and function in God's Mind. The Infinite's program for you is a roadway of positives. It must do this for It could not do otherwise, as It knows only good. The more you affirm that you are spiritual and divine, the more good happens to you.

Your mind is a directing center of life. Your mental conclusions are your only limitations. There are no shut doors and no finalities in this world. To believe that you are at the end of your road is stupid. The pathway is endless and you are a free agent. The action of God is not limited to any group, church denomination or ritual. It is limited only by your capacity to think in terms of what you want, instead of continuing your contemplation of what you do not want.

New ideas are the key to new experiences. Saying that success, true love or perfect health have passed you by only means that you have let it go past. It means you did not have a creative mental attitude to hold it in your experience. You can change every situation in your life for the better once you have decided to do it and seek a spiritual means of doing it. The Mind of God is seeking to find those of Its creation who are willing to release the past, live in the present with new ideas and plan a creative future for themselves.

In 1932 in the depths of the world depression a woman came to see me who was almost destitute. She

The Necessity of Creative Ideas

pled with me to show her a way of changing her consciousness so she could again have prosperity and freedom in money. The only question I asked was "What is the one thing above all others that you would like to do?" Her reply was that she had always wanted to be a pastry specialist. Remember that in 1932 she couldn't have found a job as a regular baker, let alone a specialist in fancy pastries. In those years such delicacies were rarely used.

I said to her, "Then go ahead and do it." She looked at me in complete amazement. I said, "If we together subconsciously accept the idea that you can be this, then every door will open for you to do it." She did not argue: she did not say it was impossible; she agreed with me. I gave her the following treatment:

There is no limitation in the Universal Spirit which is God. It remains forever the same. God knows neither depression nor impossibility. You are the vital outlet of Divine Ideas. You now welcome them and rejoice in them. Every limited poverty idea is now erased from your consciousness. To you is given by the Mind of God your right and perfect employment in the field you want. You accept this idea, and the Law of Mind is already in action producing it. You are free from all fear and established in all faith. God moves you forward into your successful career. Rejoice and be exceeding glad.

Both of us believed her desire to be sound, even though the world at that time would never have called it practical. In ways beyond anything the human mind would have thought possible, a noted manufacturer of flours arranged a one week pastry school at the Waldorf-Astoria Hotel in New York City. Out of thousands of applicants, she was one of those chosen. Living four hundred miles from New York, she hitchhiked to the city. Upon completing the course she was considered so unusual that she was offered a job as a pastry specialist in one of the few wealthy clubs able to survive during the depression. She has been constantly employed in that type of work at the finest clubs and hotels ever since, receiving a large salary.

Not once did she allow herself the luxury of fear, doubt or failure. She held fast to her belief that in right ways her good would come to pass because a Mind larger than her own would cause it to happen. Her constant thought was "There is a Power in me, acting through me, and acting for me which causes me to accomplish what I want." She knew that her mind was the place where the Power acted, and she kept it clear. She projected the idea with authority and allowed no one to discourage her. She realized that controlling her mind and emotions was a full time job and she never wavered for a moment.

What this woman did, you can do. God plays no favorites. God's Mind and Law are equally available to all. You can always change conditions, when you decide to do it, and follow through with the necessary disciplines of mind. You are mind in action. Even your body can only do and be what your consciousness decides. Every action and condition of your body is the result of subconscious thought action. Body is a field of response, never one of cause. It reacts, but cannot act of itself. Your sickness or health is the result of your subconscious thinking and you can always change this by introducing a new positive train of causative thinking based on a spiritual idea.

Life is the interaction of ideas. It is the play of thought and feeling upon the great screen of experience. Your combined use of thought and feeling, plus the direction you have given these, makes your

The Necessity of Creative Ideas

life what it is today. And, your use and direction of them determines your future. Consciousness is the cause of all experience. In your hands is the responsibility of living. You are a free agent in a Mind that delivers to you the exact reactions of your mental actions.

Life is spiritual activity. In the commonplace is the Spirit. It exhibits intelligence, purpose and plan. As a living soul, you have intelligence, purpose and plan.

An infinite Wisdom caused you to be born in these times. The Mind of God knew exactly what it was doing when you were born. You are a specialized creation of the Almighty. In you God has individualized God's mind, power and authority, so that you could create what you want when you want it. But most people cannot believe this. They have been conditioned by their religion to think of themselves as helpless. They never grasp the reins of life and proceed in the direction they would like to go. Either you act with authority upon your world, or your world will give you an average existence.

There is an Intelligence which arranges many things behind the outer scene, a Mind which knows exactly what to do, when to do it, and proceeds to fulfill your ideas. God is tremendous, magnificent and creative and all of It is yours. The more you rejoice in being a part of It, the more Life can enrich and benefit you. Say to yourself:

I rejoice in life. I rejoice in these times in which I live. I behold the goodness and the richness of life on every hand. I am the full Mind and Love of God in complete expression right now. I find so much in my life that is good. I know my victory over problems is certain for I know that my intelligence is a part of God.

Remember this at the end of a hard and busy day. Your fatigue is natural. You have faced and met problems. You have handled things to the best of your ability. That is all that Life requires of anyone. So be glad to be alive in these days right where you are. If you don't like your present routines, you can change them. There is never despair to one who knows this science. You sense the divinity within humanity and the answer within the question. Problems become exciting experiments, and faith is never dimmed.

There is no simple rule for a happier life. Successful living is hard work, but this hard work is simplified when you realize it takes place in your consciousness.

Life is the movement of intelligence through law and order producing what you select to have in your experience. I realize that you cannot keep your mind affirmative twenty-four hours a day. No individual can do this. However, you can take five minutes each morning to quietly and confidently do spiritual thinking.

Contemplate spiritual ideas and believe them possible for you to demonstrate. You have a right to health, peace of mind, a goodly measure of this world's goods and creative self-expression.

In your time of dedication to Truth, know that your life right now is a part of God and contains all the possibilities of full and rich living. Accept yourself as an intelligent loving expression of life. Do not think of your mistakes and failures during this period. They are unimportant to the Divine Wisdom. It knows them not and is not interested in what you might have done.

God is only interested in what you are and where you have chosen to go. You are the image and likeness of the creative power. You are an expanding, unfolding

The Necessity of Creative Ideas

consciousness backed up by the universal Mind. God wants you to be what you want to be. In your quiet thinking select your future, then accept it as normal for you, and then expect it to happen. Give thanks that all the ways and means to bring it to pass are already in action. Rest in the calm assurance that the Intelligence of God is making all things possible.

The above is self-treatment. It is establishing cause and the Law of Being will produce the effect. With this new concept firmly implanted in your mind things begin to happen. Follow through by letting changes come. Don't expect things to remain as they are. This they cannot do, for you have set in motion a powerful idea which acts with exactness in creating a new experience.

MONEY IS GOD IN ACTION

We are discussing money. The people who have it, want more; the people who don't have money, want it. There isn't a person in the world who will admit having too much money, and who would not like to juggle his stocks and bonds to have a little more.

What is this money that we are discussing? We worry about its valuation. We have a curious mixture of doubt and fear in most of our thought of money. We seem to be confused. We do not know whether its value is dependent upon money, as gold, locked underground in Fort Knox, Kentucky, or whether it is dependent upon the stock market. That, too, seems to affect money. And, we worry when other nations devaluate their currency for fear it will affect our own country's money. So, I think it would be a good idea if we discussed money and cleared our thought regarding it.

The last one hundred years have brought about what is called a scientific age.‡ This scientific age has given us a great deal, but the average person considers it merely in terms of their own increased personal comfort. The sincere student of science discovers that back of this increased comfort there should also be an increased understanding of the world, and of the Universe of which this planet is only a small part. One of the things, which our friends in the scientific field have done, is to make us realize that the universe is a

---

‡ *Editor's Note*: Barker is writing in the 1950s.

fluidic creation; it is an eternally flexible creation. It is always in a state of flux; it never stops or stands still for an instant. It is energy forever expanding itself. It is Intelligence forever finding new outlets for its own creative action.

As we view this Universe of infinity, eternity, and activity, and consider our planet in relationship to this great cosmic order, we behold a universal field of right action. We might say that the first necessity for understanding the world in which we live is to understand it on the premise that it is activity; it is never static. See yourself in a fluidic universe, a flexible universe, a universe that is forever in process of change, yet at the same time forever dominated and guided by a basic Intelligence, which is forever producing new forms, new creations, new experiences, all of which when seen rightly are good. If you can realize that, then you will deal with your Universe as a flowing thing. Then, you will deal with your prosperity as a flowing thing. You will immediately realize that the average person has stopped their own prosperity because they have concluded that prosperity is money in the bank, or prosperity is money in investments, instead of seeing prosperity as a flowing thing, an inlet and an outlet of activity.

There is a universal pulse-beat. This great flowing, pulsating universe has its own measurements of stars and atoms, its own pulse-beat. You, as an individual, speaking of you now physically, have your own pulse-beat which denotes to the nurse or the doctor the tempo of your circulatory system, but remember that it is a circulatory system; it is an eternal movement taking place in you. In a well person this circulation is in balance, always in right relationship. When your pulse is taken, no matter whether it is fast, slow or average, it is an indication of the tempo of your circulation. Likewise there is a barometer, if we wish to call it that, for our national pulse-beat in economics. Many people pick up their morning or evening newspaper, and the first thing they read is the stock market page, the barometer of the pulse-beat of the financial day as it has been recorded. If the market goes down, they moan; if it goes up, they rejoice. They have become dependent upon a set of statistics presented to them by authorities in the financial field for their feeling of prosperity. I am giving you these pulse-beats, because each is indicative of circulation. The stock market is dependent upon buying and selling. It is a circulatory thing, just as the pulse of your own body is dependent upon the beating of your heart, the circulatory system and the moving of the blood throughout your body. All life is circulation.

When I begin to fear lack, and that often happens, I immediately begin to work on my own consciousness, not with the question of how can I make more money, but with the question, "What do I need to do to have money circulating in my world?" For, prosperity is the circulation of money in my world. It is movement, it is an activity, it is a flow. I have often defined prosperity as being a state wherein I am always able to do what I want to do at the instant of time that I want to do it. In other words, if all the people attending a metaphysical lecture had sufficient money in their pockets to place a generous contribution in the offering plate and they had sufficient money in their pockets to have transportation home, then at that instant they would be prosperous, despite what their bank account revealed, because they would have what they needed to have to do the thing they wanted to do at the instant they wanted to do it.

The older theologies have been telling us for as long as any of us can remember that money is a dangerous thing, that money is an evil thing, and that money is a sinful thing. In metaphysics we do not believe that. But, there are countless good people who believe it, and I look at them in amazement, for while they believe that money is the root of all evil (which is not what Jesus said), they are forever bothering their employers for a raise. If you believe that money is evil, then why work for it? Why use it? Merely go and live with some kind relatives and you won't need to bother about it.

Money is a vital part of the necessary circulatory system of this age. As it is a necessity for the economic health of all of us, it must be a spiritual idea. The moment you shift your attention from the concept that money is evil, to the belief that money is wonderful, you will begin to have a greater circulation of money in your life. Anything we love increases, and anything we criticize moves out of our lives. The first step toward abundance is to love money. Why? Because it is the means which God is using at the present instant to maintain a circulation in your world of economics. But, it must be a circulation. Therefore, watch out before damming it up, hemming it in or putting a fence around it, because the joker is still in that deck of cards. If you die one of these days, your relatives have a free-for-all with it. That is the joker for people who hoard money.

Circulation is necessary to my body if I am to keep on living. Circulation is necessary in the general field of economics, if we are to have a healthy financial structure in this nation and in the world. Therefore, I can assume that circulation is necessary in my own bank account, in my own pocketbook, and more than that in my mental attitude about money. I must believe that I am in a universe which is self-sustaining. If I am in a universe which is self-sustaining, then I must be a part of it, and the creative process which causes the universe to be self sustaining must likewise be in my affairs and cause my affairs to be self-sustaining.

The universe is saying to the mind of each person, that if they will be wise in their use of money, if they will be receptive to the idea of money, they will have money. For, no good thing is withheld from those who love God, and money is good, but you have to believe that money is good. So, correct your thought about money.

Next, we must be willing to live in a state of financial flux. We must be willing to live in a state of financial flexibility and meet it without fear. If we can do that we will have more money. If only there were doctors of money, as there are doctors of bodies and doctors of the mind, for we need to be reminded often that we must be flexible in money matters. When the barometer on our bank account goes down, it is merely an indication that it will go up again, if we remain open to the idea of money.

You must sell yourself on money as a spiritual idea until it becomes an automatic subconscious pattern with you. You will find that the people who have the greatest freedom in money are the people who no longer have to think about money. They have arrived at a subconscious conviction that they will always have it. And, they always do have money, because they are subjectively convinced of the fact. The people, who have trouble in regard to money, have not yet convinced themselves that they can live in this world and have the freedom and use of money. I do not mean millions of dollars; I mean enough to live more than comfortably.

You are going to say, "But, doesn't money come from work?" The answer is "No." There are business executives who work only two hours a day, or one day a week, and take a six weeks vacation whenever they desire, and yet they receive their enormous salaries from work. They receive their money because they are considered to be worth that much money. And, the reason they are considered to be worth this much, is that they have convinced themselves that they are worth it. When you are convinced that you are worth more money walk up to your employer and say you want a raise, and you will receive it. But you will never get a raise if you merely want a raise, but are not convinced that you are doing a better job than you did a year ago; that you are willing to watch the time clock less, and that you are willing to be more active on the job. You will get your raise only when you are convinced in your own subconscious that you are worth it.

We must first convince our own minds. That is probably why every time that people came to Jesus and needed his help, he asked them, "Do you believe?" If they said, "Yes," he said, "All right, it is done." Why? Because they had arrived at a point of self-conviction and it was their own self-conviction which made the demonstration. Jesus could feed 5,000 people because he was convinced he could feed 5,000 people. He knew he could do it, so he did it. You don't know that you can do it, so you had better not try to do it. And, don't infer that the scriptural story of the feeding of the 5,000 is allegorical, or that it is a myth, for you won't know that until you have arrived at the same point of subconscious conviction which Jesus had realized.

Money is a subjective conviction on the part of the individual.

Accept the idea of money and say, "All right, it is God's Idea of circulation— (That is our definition— Money is God's Idea of circulation)—I now subjectively accept the Idea of money. I accept this Divine Idea without limitation. I do not think of money in terms of any set amount. I think of it in terms of plenty to maintain me in ease and freedom of action."

The reason that I suggest that you don't treat in terms of amounts is that wealth is a relative thing, and one fact about the Universal Mind is that it always gives plenty and to spare. I am weary of having just enough to meet my current bills. I want a little to spare. All right, that is the way the Universal Supply works. The Universal Intelligence works under a law of abundance without a secondary law of limitation. But, most individuals attempt to work under a law of abundance, with an unconscious pattern of limitation. So, they do not have results. On the surface they say that they desire plenty of money, but their subconscious pattern is $60.00 a week. As the subjective pattern has more power than the temporary conscious mind desire, they demonstrate $60.00 a week, while they could be demonstrating as much more as God wanted them to have. The Universe takes us at our valuation, and each one of us needs to increase the consciousness of our own valuation in money. As we do this, money starts to appear in our experience.

All spiritual treatment is an action of the conscious on the subconscious. Treat this way, "Money is God's Idea of circulation. This Idea, I accept. This Idea, I now accept as the basis of all my financial affairs. I like money. I believe that it is God's Activity, that it is good. I use it with wisdom. I release it with joy. I send it forth without fear, for I know that under a Divine Law, it comes back to me increased and multiplied." If you will use this treatment, and subjectively accept it, you will be amazed at the results.

Money is a Spiritual Activity. It is good, it is wonderful, and we should love it. It is not filthy lucre, it is not sinful, it is not the devil's playmate—it is God in action. The stock market is a financial barometer. We do not condemn it, we do not criticize it, neither do we bless it, we merely leave it alone. We use it as an orderly part of our business world. We do not worry about the value of dollars because whether values go up or down, we, who are convinced within ourselves that we are worth plenty of money, will always have it.

We will always have money, because the law of prosperity is based on the perpetual circulation of God's Ideas in the Infinite Mind.

This great circulation of thought is pouring into our consciousness and appearing in our world as cash on hand. This process goes on eternally, despite the value of a dollar or the value of a pound sterling. But, the people who believe that their money is dependent upon the stock market, or believe that their money is dependent upon valuation, or believe that their money is dependent upon hours of work, those people are living under the bondage of limitation, and they do not demonstrate money. They demonstrate more worry, more watching, more fear, because that is where they have placed their attention. That is where they are setting up cause, so they reap a similar effect, because cause and effect are one.

If I devote my entire thinking, which is the creative power in my world, to worry about money, then the effect must be like unto the cause, and I only have more worry about less money. That is completely logical as well as completely true. Therefore, it is necessary to take my attention from money as a necessity of life, and think of it as a God-given Idea for life as a necessary part of the normal circulatory system of the present age. Say, to yourself, "Isn't money wonderful. I'm going to release it with joy. I refuse to worry, for there is plenty more money for me."

I want to close this discussion with a specific mental treatment for money. I want you to be clear on this one idea. I am not giving you a treatment to increase your salary, I am treating for money. After you read, and declare audibly, this treatment for money, you must be willing to take it when it comes. If someone stops you on the street and invites you to a fine restaurant—go. Let your money come from any direction. I have known people who came to our Practitioners' offices for a money treatment, and after the treatment was given they would go out and mingle with a group of friends. I would hear a friend say to one of them, "May I take you to lunch?" And he would say, "Oh no, I couldn't accept." Then why should he take a Practitioner's time to treat him for money? If someone says to you, "I want to give you something," and it is at all usable, take it. If it isn't usable, take it anyway and give it to someone else, because that is the way bridge prizes circulate.

Remember, that if money is God in Action, if it is a Spiritual Idea in your life, then you should welcome with joy anything resembling it. Be a little enthusiastic about money. Don't criticize anyone who has it. If you believe that someone down the street is getting money dishonestly—what of it? They are working under the law of their own negative mind and they will be stopped. Don't worry about it. It is none of your business, and don't criticize them. Think of money as being God in Action, and whenever you see large amounts of money, say to yourself, "Isn't that wonderful!"

This human mind of ours has its tricks of limitations and it gives itself away every time. If I treat myself for prosperity, and go out and criticize someone else because he has plenty of money, it doesn't make sense, does it? The mental work I have done is rendered ineffective because my own criticism of money has erased its value.

You are going to like money, because it is God in Action. You are going to use it with wisdom, release it in joy and know it will return to you increased. Say to yourself, "Wait a moment—I always have had enough money to meet my needs and the Infinite Spirit is not going to stop my income at this point. There is no blockage in the universal system; the universe is always in a state of flux. If there is a block in the flow of money in my life, it must be a temporary human block which I have within my own consciousness. I now break that block. I accept money, appreciate money, use money and shall never again be afraid of money."

A SPIRITUAL MIND TREATMENT FOR MONEY

I now subconsciously accept this treatment. There is only one Creative Cause, God. There is only one Mind, God. There is only one Life, God. There is only one Substance, God. This present universe is the Glory of God. It is a moving, flexible, fluidic creation. It is alive with the Life, the Abundance, and the Richness of God. I abide in prosperity. Mind created me in order that It might act through me. Therefore, I am receptive to Its abundance. I am receptive to Its circulation in my life in the form of money. Money is God's Idea of circulation in my world of finance. I accept this Idea completely. I appreciate this Idea; I like it. Money being God in Action, is absolute good, it is wholesome. It is a blessing to each of us, and I am now prospered with it. I have no fear of lack for I believe that I have plenty of money. It is God's Activity in my world. It is God's Activity in my bank account. It is God's Activity in my investments. It is God's Activity in everything to which I lay my hands. This money is flowing, this money is free. I do not attempt to lock it up. I do not put a fence around it. It is God's money, I let it flow in, I let it flow out. As I release it, I know that it comes back to me, pressed down, shaken together and running over. "The Lord is my shepherd, I shall not want." I am now free in money. I rejoice in it. I appreciate it, and I thank God for it. I have money forevermore. Amen.

A SPIRITUAL MIND TREATMENT FOR PROSPERITY

The Universe is the body of God and is a system of prosperity and order. The Mind which fashioned the Universe fashioned me out of Itself. I prosper in all my ways. My spiritual prosperity maintains me in the freedom to do what I want at the instant I want to do it. I enjoy my well-being, and I know that it shall increase and multiply. I am receptive to spiritual ideas which are doing this for me. These are my security and peace of mind.

I know all money is God in action. This frees me of guilt about money and creative finances. I use my money with wisdom and like the results. I am never self-stingy. I share my wealth with those I love and appreciate. Any limitation patterns regarding money are now released from my subconscious mind. Thus, all doors open for new sources revealed to my consciousness for permanent and expanding wealth.

I give thanks to the one Source for my financial good. I appreciate every source through which it comes to me. I know that I am centered in all the good I need and all the good I want.

Made in the USA
San Bernardino, CA
02 November 2013